A Collection of
Poems & Lyrics
by Kate Barnwell

G
Grosvenor Artist Management

First published in 2013 by

Grosvenor Artist Management

32/32 Grosvenor Street

Mayfair

London

W1K 4QS

www.grosvenorartistmangement.com

Copyright © Kate Barnwell, 2013

www.katebarnwell.com

The moral right of the author has been asserted

A CIP catalogue record for this book is available from the British Library

Front cover from an original watercolour by Evelyn Dunphy, *My Room in Collioure*

www.evelyndunphy.com

ISBN 978-0-9574980-1-3

Also available in Limited Edition hardback from www.grosvenorartistmanagement.com with a FREE CD of readings by Crawford Logan & Teresa Gallagher

Praise for 'A Collection of Poems & Lyrics'

"A remarkable achievement for the young author. Her words and poems are startlingly raw and authentic. She has drawn from a deep personal reservoir that provides us with a real emotional gem."

Ivor Davis
Former Columnist, New York Times Syndicate
Former Foreign Correspondent, The Times of London and London Daily Express

"I am on my third reading and they just get better and better. I find something new each time."

Evelyn Dunphy
Award-winning watercolourist, USA

"Confident and self-assured, both traditional and modern, there is something for everyone. It has made me rediscover the pleasures of poetry."

David Chilton
Urban Fox Media, London

"I hadn't come across Kate Barnwell before…she's the real thing!
I thought the poems were outstanding!
She is one of the few poets today who can use rhyme and formal
structure without it seeming remotely forced or constraining."

Peter Murray
Pharmaceuticals and Entrepreneur, UK

"Kate is clearly an incredibly talented young poet with insights
beyond her age…
I think of a young Sylvia Plath or in part Elizabeth Barrett Browning.
She has a strong sense of the visual and is well on her way to
integrating that successfully in her writing, for what is poetry but the
handmaiden of the mind's eye."

Michael Downend
Playwright, USA

"A sometimes funny, often fragile yet haunting collection that will
stay with the reader long after the last page has turned"

Rosemary Forgan
Television Producer

I
VOICES

I find War poetry very moving. Every November I attend the Westminster Abbey Remembrance Service. The importance of remembering the past Wars has never been more relevant. The memorials, statues and monuments across London and in every town and village will always remind us of the great sacrifice of life for our country. I have stood at the base of many memorials and seen men, women and children fall silent and cry.

Tell me of England: Soldier to Mother

Tell me mother, of the grass
Is it cut? Is it green?
Are the currants ripe to pick?
It is cold here and damp and dull
But I am well

The flowers that grow in the garden
Are they reaching to the sun?
With warm faces that welcome the heat
It is dark here, no day from night
But I am well

Is the bread in the Aga sweet and tempting to touch?
Is the crust floured, the dough soft and buttered?
Did I bite too quickly?
I remember its taste, my tongue is wet
But I am well

Do the birds sing to wake the dawn?
Before the bells sound out across the green
And the branches swing their leaves in a breeze
My ears still hold those simple, dear tunes
I am well for it

Is there still a soft pillow for me to rest my head?
Where gentle words melt from mouths to nurture
From friends who hold fearless eyes
Their kind calls and simple rhymes
To make me well

Tell me mother, of England
Is She numb from pain? Is She pitied?
Does She ache from exhaustion and stumble to rise?
Does She sob to hear her children cry?
Destined to fight and destined to die
Does She feel so entirely bemused and alone
To know we now live in fields quite unknown
Dirt, disease, distance remote
All for the sake of our Island of hope.

I am so far from home
Lost my youth, yet stay well
But of old England
I say mother, please tell.

This was written after reading one of my favourite books, Frankenstein, by Mary Shelley.
The creature, which is unnamed and unloved, had the most beautiful, misunderstood soul, trapped by
a hideous appearance. Someone needed to give him words to speak and the time to listen.

The Creature's Voice

All who ever saw me cried in vain
A creature you detest, you loathe to see
It's true I am a wretched thing
Cast into shadows by people who abhor me

All I ever asked was to witness a word of love
That it might be directed to me
To chase some soft sound from your lip
I know I am an image of despair
If only you could look inside
Escape the vision, hide your pride

I am, as yet, a giving, gentle man
Who longs to gather fresh and human ways
To make myself feel the worthiness of days
To share a life, to touch a mind
To belong with other humankind

Still I hide in corners and find dark doors
I sleep in open skies, on cold, grey floors
I've watched, you see; you shape and bloom
And grow so beautifully and learn to love
Like the raven who admires the dove

But not for me, cursed, ugly face
Who possesses features that scar the soul
For I am deeply tender
With pity as my prize
Ashamed, unnoticed, vacant to the world
With envy as my vice

Is it possible to ever have love, to be warm,
To wake in the light and rise to a different dawn?
Can you offer me some relief?
Or am I given to eternal grief?

Ode to a Roman

I think I've seen my God
I think he's come to take my hand
Has he seen my great Empires
That spread across the land?

I've watched the city rise from ruins
How mighty I've become
My rivals fled in fear of me
The fields are my Kingdom

These columns stand in citadels
These temples symbolise my reign
To a glorious victory they allude
The gateways claim my name

I own all the valleys I can see
The wild lands and the shore
The heart of all the fruitful lands
Which we dispute for evermore

If my power wavers
I shall have no fear
My foes find feuds and conflicts
Whenever they draw near

But tonight is different
And history will write my fate
My comrades who worship me
Turn their love to hate

The revolution has evolved
I can sense a beaming light
Always watch your back my friend
For I won't last the night.

Forgive, Forget

I can forgive you, the day you lost my doll
And my bag left on the kitchen stool
I can forgive the time I was late for school
And the note you forgot to write
To say I didn't feel alright
I can forgive the afternoon you were out
And you missed my play, because you'd gone away
Or the morning I was low
I had to stay at home
And someone had to stay with me
It wasn't my fault I felt unwell
Some sign of sympathy?

But I can't forgive or understand your mind
For being so cruel and so unkind
When you stopped my mother from seeing me
Take the house, the car and keys
Don't take her from me please
And all the tears, the aching cries
Mostly kept knotted up inside
And painful weekly sad goodbyes

I won't forget how she fought for me
And how you lied, how everyone lied
And made up some absurd disguise
To undermine her love and care
Yet with one clear kick the courts made rules
Bribed, befuddled archaic fools
To satisfy the final blow
That I must stay and she must go
The strange way people behave
So many nights I was strong and brave

I sometimes think how young I seemed
Those haunted nights and frightening dreams
It was the section of my past
That after years of fighting could not last
And we were reunited thankfully
Yet still it troubles me
And it is this I must live with
But what you did I won't forget
And I can't and won't forgive.

Leaving Me

They told me she was sick
And she was strong
And I was not
Brave and stoic
And heroic.
It would not be long
I was numb
Would I become
The only one
To sit alone and talk?
It was a thought
I did not see come.
And all the years
We came to share
There is no memory
Without her there
Way up front or close behind
In the pictures of my mind
And now she tidies just the same
No aches or pains
No pleasures gained.
But this is such a heavy blow
To know
Someone comes to tell you so

It's very nearly time to go
It's never right, it's never fair
To leave before you're ready
To glance at faces in despair
However steady.
So relieve her from the fear
A simple silence stirs a tear
Wakeful nights and weary days
Become a tiring added strain.
We focus on the happy things
On family, what Spring will bring
So how can I?
See her live lively
And then soon die
Quietly
So I must be happy
Chat cheerfully
Act normal, laugh loudly
Contentment be.
Time clocks on reluctantly
Slipping by
It startles me
And softly as she fades from grace
God rests her in his blessed place.

The Blind Man

I've seen him on the corner
I see him on the street
Just because he doesn't see
Doesn't mean he cannot speak

He spoke of blue trees in his head
Of giant plants and talking birds
Of narrow alleys and crowded roads
What could he know of those?
This was his vision, he said

He doesn't want your charity
Money and pity are for the poor
He just asks for a little time
To spend a moment, no more

He shares his view of a sightless world
And imagines it so fine
Without the urban angers, the dirt
The hardened streets and city crime

He has felt the tears of joy
He has tasted sweeter fruits
He smells the cut grass in June
Hears both the owl and traffic hoot

Seldom does he grumble
Mumble or despair
But only gestures in excitement
With sparks of witty flair

He's made me look again at life
And weigh up all its woes
And find peace with others
To let things come and go

If you miss him on your busy way
I tell you he is there
For he can feel you rushing
Through your life so unaware.

A quiet moment in an English cathedral

Saints and Angels

The sun shone through the mullioned glass
It stained the cold stone
In pieces of orange, of red, green and blue
See the reflection
There on the wall
A man in deep contemplation
"Who is He?" I asked
This figure made up of glass
A dark voice from the corners claimed
The peace of the silence
Broke through with sternness, said in equal excitement
"We are told from the beginning
Of lives that hold wonders,
Those who spoke of great miracles
They were faithful and willing
They washed away sins, took journeys
Followed paths, so fulfilling."

Above our heads the angels listened
They sat carved in their kind covered niches
Weary and whispering, with warm weathered faces
With a lute that would carry a tune to the roof
The notes catching the dust in a pool of pale rays
The dark voice again cracked with sudden approach
"You may never reach such heights in this age."

But then I was left, a mortal, alone
"Who are these patches of colour, soft on the eye?"
Shamefully, solemnly I came to cry
When a child, so close, never noticed before
Had tiptoed so silently from the far north-end door
He had listened intently and knew all my thoughts
Knew all my failings, my sadness, my flaws
He knew why I came and what I sought
He knew I had sinned and I needed belief

"They are the saints, the sun shines through them,
Today they are bright; it is their light that will guide you."
I felt a rush of blood flow to my cheeks
My feet were lifted, my body less week
"You may never rise to the height of a saint."
 He said with a slanted, faint smile
And with a sparkling look, I shall never forget
The child spoke this last part with deep emphasis
"But blessed friend, value your life
Do not doubt, do not fear it
For I am your Angel
Come down to be near you."

I used to

I used to cry real tears
I used to laugh out loud
Sadly all the spark has gone
And nothing bothers me

A part of me went missing
I lack the strength to get it back
I used to act so fast
But now I'm slow, slow, slow,

There's an emptiness inside me
It's cold and dark and hard to bear
I used to feel full and peaceful
But I'm tired, nobody's there

I passed snowdrops in the graveyard
So pure and white and small
Growing pale with the morning sun
And in places we once walked

I used to gaze at jet streams
Marvellously high and strong
And make dreams over bridges
But my days like this are gone

I used to smile in spring time rain
Danced light, talked lovingly
Now I'm lonely like the boat, lost upon the sea
Or the winter swallow who forgot he had to flee

I pass houses in the street
Their windows mirror my face
I used to know life all by heart
Now my head lies somewhere else.

II
OUTSIDE

Autumn

The fresh cut fields of golden hay
The twigs entwined in bales we play
And all in the light of a long shadowed sun
The earthy scents, the day's darkness to come
Into the air, onto my tongue
Undulating clouds take their airy flight
The heat slow rising soon falls to cool night
The colours will mellow, they no longer seem bright
Soft ripening reds, dwindling green grasses
Burnt to the touch, the corn plump as we grasp it
Every little bird, new butterfly and bee
Will dance in the meadows left wild and free
Lifted in peace, season's calm company
I sit with this sight to feel it soothe me.

Night-time Blackbird

When the sun has slowly set and darker hours loom
Local to his homely bed, the blackbird sings his tune
Loud and pompous, deeply strong, throaty to the core
Heard wide above the downstairs noise, the frequent raucous roar.

In response a fellow friend will join in all the chat
Together in their rightful turns discussing more of this than that
To me it adds essence to a very lonesome day
To think that on the sunset hour these birds have much to say

Perched high upon a chimney top or the tallest cherry tree
I wait to share in all their stories, the two of them and me
Notes are swallowed, spoken, sung clear before night's rest
Then ready to return to their twisted, twiggy nests

I walk away, as they fluff their feathers out to fly
Muttering and cheering their last beakful of goodbye
I ponder, mindful of the things they chose to say
That run like little melodies to mark the close of day.

Seascape

Settling out at sea and nestled in the sky
A cloud with peachy softness moves
Above the deep and darkening blues
Looming high and spreading wide
Shaping and moulding its gathering size

The milky shadows form across the sea
And greys of every palate splash and blend
And view the great divide
The heavy scattering of rain
The showy splashes stain and soak the contours
As distant creamy colours wash away
And stormy patterns persevere
To whip up the winds that twist and pull
That push on heaving, weighty skies

They hover over grassy cliffs to breathe it green
To make it wild and tempered, fresh and clean
Winds will whisper their way into a breeze
Stretching the trees and teasing the leaves
Floating carelessly over the gentle scene
Humbling the modest land
This inward flight finds some relief
As troubled currents slowly cease

Down below, where the beaches spread
The tide draws back its forceful strike
Reveals the pools of little worlds
The rocks, the pebbles, the hidden caves
The playful lives unfurl, unafraid

And me, where I serenely sit
Amongst the peace, in tranquil state
To gaze at beauty with open eye
To watch its changing moods, its mystery
Out at sea and in the sky.

Stars

Supernova particles of dust
On which To make our wishes
All those millions of miles away
A black galaxy of floating, dazzling Rocks
Silent by day, by night, an audience of
STARS

I wrote this sonnet in 2012 aged 32 as a dedication to William Wordsworth whose sonnet 'Composed on Westminster Bridge' was written in 1802 when he was 32. With the passing of history that Westminster Bridge and London have seen, the sight is both changed and yet timeless.

What Words are Worth

Morning shakes off the dirty dark of night
Mesmeric eyes gaze, summoned by splendour
All the stages of the day yet unstirred
Each quarter booms, it echoes far reaches
The light leans in to blanket the features
A freshness falls to old and new pierced skies
To reach gracious and proud, its soul survives
The sites still stand secure in their triumphs
And the water powers the river flow
Breaking, breathing out on the banks below
With unstill sureness, frantic pulses sound
To generate warmth, to flourish surrounds
Sleepy boats bobbing as the streets soon pound
Why every sigh belongs to me, London found.

III
LOVE

Soft Words

From every kiss you gave me, every look you passed to me
I felt my heart lift and my face smile
And all the while you were away
I prayed for the next day
When you would come back for me
And I could tell you how missed you'd been
Your voice, your hands, your heart-shaped lips
To whisper how hard life can seem
As I watch you hold me in my dreams
Longing for you to say slowly
That I need never leave and you would never go
I will feel warm again; your soft words will never end
And you would fend for me, take on what was unforeseen
Let clouds close on this melting scene
Where you show with all honesty
How we were meant to be.

You may never come to realise
What you have made me be
I am a dreaming soul sublime
Whose heart is lost to thee

Heart and Head

Love has come into my head
Risen from the heart to sit with sense
But sense asks questions
It doubts feelings and beauty
It finds ways to fault
And ways to fear and ways to fluster
Love never has to reason, to consider
To consult, it just comes and with it
All that is good, and young and pure and pleasing
That settles later into quiet understanding and comfort
For now, head will only berate its growth
And love may fail to find its feet
To fuel its wondrous tendrils
Held back by common sense and dignity
Restrained by decorum and caution
The stubbornness of head whose object and safety comes
In quashing soft and gentle thoughts
In controlling all that is wild and untamed
That is new and unsearched
Live only by the heart, surrender to its signs
Let it converse kindly with head's calculations
Taking risks, having fun, no deliberations
Use the two
To make love's dreams come true.

When love is gone

How can I live beyond a day?
When love is gone
If I am left to find a way
When little lies beyond

How can I breathe sweet, warm air?
When love is gone
If I do not have the time to care
When hours seem long

How can I feel wholly complete?
When love is gone
If each task's a tiring feat
When I want to belong

How can I rest in sleeping?
When love is gone
If I lose my sense to weeping
When I should carry on

How can anybody understand?
Now love is gone
The coldness of my hand
The numbness of my heart
The loss in sunken cheeks
The weakness of my soul
The bleak colours of dawn and dusk are drawn
The awkwardness of my walk
The tremble of unspoken thought

How can I live beyond a day?
Now my love has gone.

Never go to Paradise alone

I walked the shores, they felt so smooth
The warm winds blew, my body cooled

The smells and sounds just filled the skies
I sensed a teardrop round my eyes

The salty waters were clear and blue
I sat under palms, watched sunrise too

I swam in currents with jumping fish
I dived below to make a wish

Never go to paradise alone I said
This beauty must be shared instead

My sandy toes and my hardened feet
A local drum with intermittent beat

The captive view of a white stretched beach
The sailing boats beyond my reach

The darkest sky with beaming moon
The echo of a distant tune

The shining stars, dazzle bright
I felt Earth moving through the night

The sparkle and shimmer of tiny fish
I looked to the pools to make my wish

Never go to paradise alone, I said
Return with your loved one, instead

Show to them the purple sky
Exotic birds as they fly by
How the sun will warm your face
In winter I discovered this place
I've chosen it for you and me
Contented by a view of sea
Happy and smiling I suffice
Upon this Isle of Paradise.

I said to her

I said to her, of course I love you
Of course I care
And she questioned further
And my cries became small murmurs.

I said to her, that all my thoughts
Are good and they belong to her
And she pondered, she contemplated
And my sighs were miscalculated.

I said to her, how fair and fine
And wonderful she is
And when she smiles, she beguiles me
And my words fell flat and silently.

I said I've seen how the light
Shines upon her face
And there within her soul
And how only she can radiate
With grace and beauty that fascinate.

I said to her, to dry her tears
I held her close
Dispelled the fears
And rising from a saddened state
Desperate questions of lovers' debate.

I stood by her, as I always do
And I said to her,
Of course I love you.

Stuck in Song

I saw you today but I can't say hello
I'm too shy to greet you and tell you so

I've taken a walk through time and through space
And yet where you stand is the hardest place

I imagine long days of immeasurable bliss
How much of the day is spent thinking like this

I gathered with crowds and stared at you there
I've waited at doors, sat in rooms if I dare

I sent you letters then flowers divine
And wishing for you as eternally mine

But now you've become so wanted, I find
Harder to reach, and of me, still so blind

In a song I can choose all the best words
Perhaps you will listen, and I will be heard

But you have another somebody there
Who takes your hand and ruffles your hair

And if someday you do turn to me
For I never left this spot you see

And with all your love and modesty
For passions drive us senselessly
In this world so great to be
Not fractured, but show fragility
And have honour in humility

So lean in and listen for there is a tune
Dancing in the open sky, beyond a yellow moon

But what will you know and what will you care?
My words stuck in song are lost to the air.

Pink skirt, Blue shirt

Everyday I come to notice them
They meet, will greet and stroll along as friends
The lady in the pink skirt, the man in the blue shirt
He is tall, soft in step at her side
She is light, gentle and somewhat shy
His manners are thoughtful, careful and considered
With kindly smile and slanted slender face
She responds with bashful look and lowered head
He picks a flower as an excuse to touch instead
She knows he deserves a hand to hold
Yet an assumption on his part would be too bold
But in time she will warm and turn to him
Her confidence will be quick to come and grow
He must be committed to her mood
And so with each occasion these two improve

I saw it once in me, when I fell in love
And all because I took, I gave the time
One day the pink skirt will be lacy white
And the blue shirt will turn to darker suit
Vows exchanged and life arranged
A strong and lasting love in these two
I saw it once in me, when I fell in love
And all because I took, I gave the time
For her, for us to let happiness be
Pink skirt, blue shirt
Good luck to you, from me.

I realise

If I had only one day
I would sit and watch you breathe
I realise, I never did it before
There were always other demands

If I had only one day
I would turn to see your face
I realise, I was too busy to see
So time rolled on, moments fell shy

If I had only one day
I would listen to you talk
To realise, how softly you speak
And watch words just melt from your lips

If I had only one day
I would make you feel special
I realise, I was never really there
As every day just passed away

If I had only one day
I would hold and hug you gently
I realise, I never touched you enough
Arms were brushed and kisses gone

If I could have one more day
I would show you more of life
I would offer you everything
I realise each new year went: wasted

I realise now, as I am gone to my sleep
A single bird comes to sing
To offer the comfort and relief
That I can never bring

So when he's gone to winter
And you alone can quietly sleep
I realise, my promise to care was lost
And why you can only weep.

In this poem I imagined a man (now dead) gazing down in spirit at his aging wife. He recalls briefly their life and romance before promising that she need not fear death and that they will be reunited. I think this reassurance needed a poem.

Watching on

As you stop to find each step more the effort still
And solace in the close of the day
And careful pride in matters and words to say
So the flow of passing years is weary with its will

How much I wish to gaze upon the opening of your eye
The way I read a single furrow or manner from your face
Or enter in to find your homely, gentle ways of grace
Your step upon the wooden floors as soft sounds skirt by

Did we not take the beauty in life?
Always to laugh and play in its great surrounds
To feel as if the skies were coloured only for us
And mountains grew with each smile we saved
The rustle in the woods and the whispers that we braved
The sun in which we danced, the dark days kept indoors
Or the sorry tears that fell for no accord
To be different was to be rarely understood

When it is your time to come to me
For I shall forever wait
A promised place soothes pain and fear
It solves our end of days
I'll come to meet you, take your hand
For you need not be afraid.

In fiction and in life there are characters we come across with lasting love stories. It may be love at first sight or it may take time to grow. Here I imagine the gentleness of a man and the soft submissive delicacy of a woman, coming together. This poem was inspired by the image of heroes and heroines in history and novels and the subject of a kiss depicted in so many works of art.

Dreaming of a kiss

He, like the proud lion, saw her standing there
But, unlike the lion, he was not a beast to tear
His eyes fixated, feasted, and stared
With soft paw steps he made modest moves
And soon stood beside her, tall and graceful
She turned in a single breath of kindest faith
Here a thousand words were read between them
An approach that seemed so natural, so unrehearsed
Of which poets write and draft in verse
He silenced all heady thoughts, reached down
Her quiet acceptance was wooed and found
A kiss that could seal and read a soul
It searched, it conquered, so gained its place
And served to overcome the great image of his face.

IV
COMEDY

The other side of the bed: Mrs Wren

When one night, all tucked up in bed
The candles waxing above their heads
The fire lit a wholesome hearth
Windows shuttered from winter draughts
Distant muttering, and faintly laughs
Carried in the street, out in the dark

Mrs Wren leaned to her husband to say
"You've been so awfully quiet today
What's on your mind, what's in your head?"
And with gushing answer he simply said
"I'm sorry I've been so very aloof
What troubles me most is this mighty roof
I'm planning a dome of such enormous size
Breathtaking, bulbous, a balloon in the sky
It must, it will, catch a wandering eye
Its scale shall make our London cry
'How impressive, how simply grand'
My dear people will flock to see it stand
Along the Thames the ships will cheer us
Our jealous friends jeer and fear us
With perfect balance, looming power and poise
Stretching and rising above whirling noise

An earthly symbol of Majesty to mankind
A rightful place for peace, for prayer divine
With classical proportions, serenity and grace
An interior with columns and heavenly space
It must shock, delight, inspire and thrill
Designed with precision, care and skill."

"Oh my dear" said Mrs Wren
"It's late, but you must take up your pen
Make designs, sketch and draw
Build it better than all before
Give us an emblem to shout about
Look to your name and do not doubt
For when it be done, it will be called
My Christopher Wren's Great St Paul's."

Why?

Why is the bee so busy, has he got so much to do?
What if he is sick and comes down quick with flu?

Why does the wind whistle; when all of us can speak?
What is it thinking, what does it seek?

Why do leaves fall in autumn? And so the tree stands bare.
It needs a warm coat in winter, so it isn't really fair.

How come when you scratch an itch you can cause a scratch?
Where does an itch come from as a matter of fact?

Does left know there's a right or are they foes?
Did they fight; turn around some very long time ago?

Why do bells ring, choirs sing, pianos play a tune?
For bells can toll, choirs can chant, roses bloom in June.

If you can't answer questions, will you ever know?
If you never travel, where do you go?

Everyday I find a query, I'm yearning to learn more
Teach me what you can, it need not be a chore.

There's so much to talk about, share it with a friend.
You can start at the beginning but you'll never reach an end.

Grandma's teatime

Sophie won't touch the chocolate, it makes her put on weight
Frank is at the dentist, and is always running late
Auntie has an allergy to flowers, cats and cake
Bob prefers the sweets to the savouries I make
But nothing with an icing or frosting on the top
Keep the scones away from Jack; he's sure to eat the lot
There are two, no three, types of the plumpest homemade jam
Buttered buns, flans and pies, sandwiches with ham
And plenty without a sniff of meat to please the vegan Jan
There's tea with milk, squash and juice, coffee with single cream
The recipe for sponges holds not a trace of margarine
The jellies and fruit salad, I chose to save till last
Good to keep a quiet reserve when appetites act fast
The plates are clean, the table set, the napkins pressed and dry
Oven warming nicely as time goes ticking by
Calm before demanding kids come rushing through the door
Causing all commotion, waking the dog up from the floor
He will benefit from bits of crumb as the gobbling begins
A crust of pastry, upturned roll, discarded ginger thins
However much preparing, the family come round
With all the fuss and banter and jolliness of sound
I know I'd never want it any other way
They are forever all my world, come to me this day.

Train journey mobile phone

I don't want to listen to your conversation on the train

How you drain the concentration from my preoccupied brain

I'm not interested in hearing of your awful day at work

How you put in all the hours, how your headache's getting worse

We know you'll be at the station at a quarter after five.

Yes the car is ready it's been mended and is fine

Your son is feeling better, he had a day off school

But we clearly get the message you're not an easy one to fool

The plumber came at 10am and sorted out the leak

We heard it's taken at least six or seven weeks

The bill for the holiday has finally come through

Funny how it starts at one price and then just grew

The music in the carriage is registering too loud

Eventually you'll be rid of this unrelenting crowd

Tomorrow will be just the same back up on the train

Coming home late, wet umbrella from the rain

So my friend, so close indeed

Please save us from this rant

We're almost home at last

Can I be more frank?

So leave your conversation, kindly at the door

Before we all shout loud and clear, you're really such a BORE!

Sock

I dropped a sock upon the stair
But today it wasn't there
It was nice and clean, it didn't smell
It fell from the pile but couldn't yell
It's supposed to be safe inside a drawer
Not discarded on the floor
Perhaps tomorrow I might find
It sitting with its fellow kind

So during the day, when I was out
It found its voice to bravely shout
I'm bright and spotty with a yellow rim
Search me out before the day turns dim
I was mixed up with the scarves and hats
And pounced upon by friendly cats
Surrounded by a pile of books
No one found the time to look
Get up from your chair I'll call
Is there anybody there at all?
And maybe soon I'll make a pair
If I'm *not* left hanging on the stair.

The Weather of Seasons

Never have the British enjoyed a better day
When discussing our Island's weather in a perambulating way
It's been the hottest summer since the record books began
Only in the south of course not north of Birmingham
The beach shops were busy selling us the tat
Which in one month is useless, sitting limp with this and that
There are those that spend the holiday soaking up the sun
With very little clothing, what have these girls become?
The gardeners have been sweating waiting for the cool
To water in the evening is a well known green-man's rule
Outdoor dining under parasols becomes a thrill one thinks
We dip berries in thick cream and make ice to chill the drinks
There's the smell of burning charcoal or the cutting of the grass
Tunes of soulful music sing from open windows as you pass
The atmosphere is lazy and every task is left till late
For hot summers are so special and how long we have to wait.
Then one day out you go to buy your loaf of bread
To find the air is different, there's a cooler wind instead.
The spiders spin their webs and leaves are turning brown
Their edges tend to curl and fall crisp upon the ground
We pull out extra layers and comment on the grey
Sit closer to the heaters and watch bushes bend and sway
The apples and the pears sit neat in buttered pies
We thought of doing sewing but it gave us tired eyes

We've packed away the flip flops and replaced them quick with boots
We shall not fear the muddy climb of any neat pursuits.
And then the days are shorter, we lose an hour to the dark
The bony woodlands steeped in brown, unfulfilled and rather stark
Yet there still remains one debate – it divides us in to sorts
Those who love the pure white snow, it melts in all their thoughts
And those who of its mention fall sad and so forlorn
At the prospect of it freezing up the drive and round the lawn.
Someone spends cold days sorting out the pipes
Then running up a hefty sum of freezer-friendly wipes
We must start each Monday morning of another winter week
Without a sigh, a groan, or a painful sore upon our feet
The only hope is spring and what it promises to bring
A swathe of fresh green splendour and birds that charm and sing
Lovely buds and nice new shrubs, bulbs and blossoms too
Fewer frosts to stun the crops, just gentle morning dew.
The tides are high the sun is low, the church bells ring afar
The gardens slowly start to glow, we leave backdoors ajar
To creep out early in the morning with a cup of tea
Pick up the milk and biscuits with the paper on your knee
Every season comes to touch us and its weather we endure
How the British love to mutter, mumble, moan, forever more
But this favoured pastime puts a smile upon their face
The weathered theories and solutions of this happy human race.

A coffee kind of guy

I'm the girl who drinks tea
So what's he gonna see in me?
If he's a coffee kind of guy
We can get by, if we try

I like the morning, he likes it late
He grabs a pastry, I hesitate
He'll take his bike, I get the bus
Too much rushing, too much fuss

I'll stay in bed, so he'll be out
It's the little things we never talk about
But then he holds the door, stands up for me
Calls me up, pays for dinner – occasionally

He's mostly man, but sometimes bloke
He loves to laugh, to tell a joke
With his friends he grabs a smoke
But puts it out 'cause it makes me choke

In the day, if you ever think of me
The girl who sits to drink her tea
Do not choose to pass good thoughts by
My coffee kind of guy.

In the Bakery

Sitting early on the shelf waiting for the bell
All those oozy doughnuts with a sweet and sticky smell
Through the door the children run gathering a pace
Pointing, shouting, crying out, grabbing at the space
The tongs come out and down they fly
Who will get the choicest buy?
There's apple pie and pastry swirls
The Danish buns cause quite a stir
Lemon sponges, crusty breads
The jammy faces turn some heads
But here's a child, he's awfully glum
He's indecisive, there's always one
Looking awkward, takes great care
Wants to linger here and there
To stare and make a proper choice
And so encouraged, will find his voice
"Two Chelsea buns, a French éclair"
Said with such a soulful air
And with all the joy that sugar brings
In licking cream and white icing
He'll pass by the window along the street
With eyes so wide and chocolate cheeks
Tomorrow's joy brings much the same
The baker's collection of fancy names
And those oozy doughnuts come out once more
To greet the gaze of those before

The Bard

Out in the rose garden, with some time to think
A man sits with a book, some paper and ink
A scratchy quill for a pen, and a map of the world
Gathering his ideas, whatever unfurls
With histories not made, yet some now long dead
He weaves his stories from fanciful thread
The historical writing follows closely his thoughts
Bearing poor resemblance to what we were taught
Yes Henry was great, fought battles won wars
Yet pity the king who waves the white boar
The colourful life that society can bring
The work of artistic, rich imaginings
Themes of adventure, of love and mystical plots
Confusion, cross-dressing, these scenes not forgot
From witchcraft and scheming, tragedies arise
The creation of jesters, villains; our heroes disguised
The conscience intrigues him; deception, desire
Politics, principles, all manners inspire

The fair and the mighty, such characters enthral
Indulge all our senses, give rowdy applause
To rousing great speeches, the lines well rehearsed
The sonnets and quotes, perfect prose of sweet verse
This father, an actor, then writer and poet
What stirs in his mind, why dear few can know it
A Man of his era, who lived well and quite clean
In his Garden of Eden surrounded by green
The greatest name in a time fuelled by fear
England remembers, Mr William Shakespeare.

Bustle

It's time for tea and I'll be late
Oh take me from this bustling place
I can see it now, as I wait
How every slice of jumbo cake
Soon disappears without a trace
And all the squash gone from the shelf
If I could lean in, help myself
And form an orderly lady queue
As finger buns go 2 by 2
Neatly whipped and out of view
This blessed bus when will it come
I'll have to stand till I am numb
Maybe I'll get a chocolate roll
Before the very last is sold
Or Mrs Smith's apple tart
Which really is a work of art
If he stands too close, I'll nudge his back
Or poke him with my summer hat
Off the bus and down the road
Off before the rest unload
With cheery face and glowing nose
Wait a minute, there's a note
Has the vicar found time to gloat?
Tea postponed till 4.30
'Village hall still rather dirty.'

Must be cleaned before the tea
Oh! I say, oh deary me
Twenty minutes I now must wait
And curb this hunger, for Heaven's sake
So I'll just take this small cake of mine
Perch on a bench, to be refined
I'll nibble just a corner bit
While I wait and think and sit
But all that comes into my head
Is the thought of sandwich bread
Filled with layers of savoury spread
All recipes are fearfully guarded
Amateurs will be discarded
But surely this is homely fun
A spoon of jam to fill a bun
No competition, no prize, no draws
No pointing, no picking, no finding flaws
All that matters to me now
Is tea, with a nice old crowd
A sip, a chat with some old chum
A bite, a munch of yum, yum, yum
Gathered friends and company
A welcome place where I can be
Just me.

The Cold

I hate the cold
And all the clothes I have to wear
And the blow of the breeze
That makes you sneeze
And freezes up all your toes
And tingles round your nose
I hate the cold
And the grey clouds that threaten in the sky
And the way we have to live inside
To hide from all the gloom
That nearly always looms
When you are cold and tired
And tired from the cold
A hot cup to reach and hold
And then you scauld your fingertips
Swollen sores, and drying lips
I hate the cold
I cling to heaters and run up stairs
And all the clothes I have to wear.

V
LYRICS

She's Not Me

Here I find my feet again
They walk down the same old street
Wondering if this time
By chance we just might meet

I know you've gone and made your choice
So many voices came your way
I can't believe it's you
Who forgets and turns away

Chorus:
O it's just not me
Beside you now
However hard I shout out loud
She's just not me
You turn to see

O it's just not me
Beside you now
However hard I shout out loud
She's just not me
You turn to see

When I look back to the days
There was love there for sure
Between you and me
It was worth fighting for

I think you saw me somewhere there
You're every memory
Shall I stay away?
Leave discreet and quietly

Chorus:
O where will you go?
What will you do?
How I wished I would be the one
That you took to
But she's not me…

O where will you go?
What will you do?
How I wished I would be the one
That you took to
But she's not me…

Those Days

You know those days that start off grey
Become patchy, some pouring rain
And then the sun with its rainbow rays
Shows some promise just as time starts to fade.

Is time fading on us?
Yes I was different
That's what you loved
But your thinking isn't doing
And you're doing not that much.

You know those days when nothing gets done
Everything planned, but you helpless succumb
To the times that are tough, to the pain that will come
Find me an answer to what you've become.

Is time fading on us?
Yes I was different
That's what you loved
But your thinking isn't doing
And you're doing not that much.

You know those days when you don't feel yourself
And you long to live quietly as somebody else
Because the path that you took has changed its course
And the dreams that were promised aren't there anymore.

Taken

Take each part till I am bled
I give you myself
But tell me the heart sings a song just for you
It needs
To find life,
Find hope
Bearing the painful love-strokes

My hurt will rage then find tears
My soul feels the fears
And tell this man blind in love, hopeful for time
To go
To live low
Loose faith
Cutting and killing his words

Sufferance can be so cruel
Happiness, it is for fools

If I'm alone and unfound
With throbs hard to bear
The past comes to tease my head, good words I'll plea
A call
But no sound
Just left dead on the ground

Is this the last breath I take?
So show me my fate
And tell me the end comes to choke me,
I wait
To see it's too late
No touch can heal the hate

Sufferance can be so cruel
Happiness, it is for fools.

Away From Me

There's nothing I can say
To change your mind
To make you stay

I know, you've known for long
You don't belong
You will not stay

Give me one more chance

There's nothing I can say
To change your mind
To make you stay

Chorus:
Quietly as you go
As you walk away
Tender steps cut painfully
Away, from me

Through tears, I tell myself
That you'll be safe;
Found someone else

Sad eyes and vacant face
Words fall to dust
Brushed from this place

Give me one more chance

I know, you've known for long
You don't belong
You will not stay

Chorus:
Quietly as you go
As you walk away
Tender steps cut painfully
Away, from me

Quietly as you go
As you walk away
Empty thoughts not felt before
O, as you walk away
Away from me...

All Has Been Said

There's no hope here within
A heart heaves of sin
And so slowly
Oh so slowly
This love that's wearing thin

Here you stand in disguise
The secrets and the lies
Our times in sad demise
No promise made this time
All has been said

There's a sadness inside
A lost love, a lost pride
And I'm lonely
I'm so lonely
This pain for me to hide

Not a word in my head
Not a smile to be shed
Nothing is sung, nor read
Bitter tears fall instead
All has been said

You did choose
Now its' me you must lose
So you have fled
And love is dead.

In Haven

Softly, softly now I see your face
These great skies hold such deep space
My distant long lost place

Gently, gently close your eyes make dreams
Love is found on bright sunbeams
Happy it all will seem

Carefully the wind will play
Come chase clouds that turn to grey
Hopeful love will stay

Brightly shining stars appear
Mysteries so dark yet clear
Love hides me from fear
Love hides me from fear

Love guides me, I'm here, I'm here
Love guides me, I'm here...

www.ingramcontent.com/pod-product-compliance
Lightning Source LLC
Chambersburg PA
CBHW020514100426
42813CB00030B/3240/J